Your 60 Minute Lean Business

Volume 2 - The Pillars

Your 60 Minute Lean Business
Volume 2 – The Pillars
November 2014
First Edition

ISBN: **978-1503139480**
Copyright © 2014 Jason Tisbury

All rights reserved. No part of this publication may be reproduced or transmitted in any form or by any means, electronic or mechanical, including photocopying, recording, or by any information storage and retrieval system, without the written permission of the author, except where permitted by law.

Also by Jason Tisbury:

Your 60 Minute Lean Business:
5S Implementation Guide
Total Productive Maintenance
Standardized Work
Kaizen Mindset
JIT
Jidoka
Volume 1 – The Foundations

7 Steps To A Lean Business

Foreword

Your 60 Minute Lean Business – Volume 2 is a collection of the books five and six in the series. This volume, titled The Pillars contains the complete individual books titled:

- JIT – Just in Time Implementation Guide
- Jidoka

Why pillars? When looking at the lean house, you will see it consists of the foundations, the pillars and the roof. The foundations of 5S, TPM, Standardized Work and Kaizen Mindset were discussed in Volume 1 The Foundations. The pillars of Just in Time and Jidoka are critical next steps in the lean journey.

This volume has been put together to keep the pillars together. Each of the included titles can be read in around 60 minutes. Why 60 minutes? Well for a couple of reasons. It occurred to me a number of years ago while searching through libraries and book stores for texts on the topic of lean manufacturing and lean business that most of the available books were quite large and often not easy to understand for someone new to the topic. The essence of lean is to remove waste from a business and its processes, yet here were all of these books that were filled with non-essential words – waste. I felt a book on the topic of lean should itself be lean. With this in mind I went about writing my first book on lean – 7 Steps To A Lean Business – an overview of lean manufacturing and lean business systems.

At 140 pages, this book can be read in a couple of hours and while the details may not enable one to immediately turn a business lean, I believe 7 Steps does provide a very sound overview and ground learning for the lean newcomer.

Now it is time to share the details of some of the different lean tools, I started writing a book detailing all of the tools but soon realised what I was writing wasn't lean enough. And so the Lean Business in 60 Minutes idea was conceived.

If you are a business owner or manager and are looking for a concise, detailed guide to implementing a Lean Business System, then this book was written especially for you. My goal is to share what I have been lucky enough to learn with other like minded people who may not have had the dumb luck that I have had. When I say dumb luck, I mean dumb luck. The following is the story of how I came to learn lean, I'm sharing this story to firstly build my credentials and secondly to show how anybody can learn and implement these tools.

At the age of 32 I was working in a factory after a recent business failure when I was lucky enough to break two fingers in a ten ton press. It was quite a bad break, twelve months recovery including two surgeries (one bone graft). Now it may seem strange to call that lucky, but luck is what you make of a situation. Even though I had only one working hand, I could still use a computer, and I was fairly handy on a computer (pun not intended). I ended up working with the Quality Manager who by chance was starting to implement some lean manufacturing / continuous improvement ideas in the business. I learnt a great deal during this time. I was also lucky that this company was in the automotive industry and that one of their main customers was Toyota, probably the best company in the world to learn from. I spent the next five years living and breathing the Toyota Production System (TPS) with direct instruction and mentoring through Toyota. Now after having implemented lean systems and tools through a variety of companies in many organisations in many diverse industries, it is time to share what I have learnt for others to benefit.

Your 60 Minute Lean Business

Just In Time

Contents

WHAT IS JUST IN TIME?	9
1. TAKT TIME	11
2. LOAD LEVELING	16
3. THEORY OF PULL PRODUCTION	22
4. KANBAN	32
5. VISUAL MANAGEMENT	42
6. PULLING IT ALL TOGETHER	48
7. SOME MORE TOOLS	52

What is Just in Time?

Lean Business

Jidoka – Quality

Just In Time

Standardised Work	Kaizen
5S	TPM

Just in time is one of the pillars of the lean house and is a critical element of a lean business. Just in Time (JIT), when deployed correctly will reduce inventory requirements and the cost of poor quality by maintaining a flow of parts/materials in line with the production requirements. This will reduce the impact of many of the 7 wastes:

- Walking
- Overproduction
- Rework
- Motion
- overProcessing
- Inventory
- Transport

There are a number of elements of a successful JIT system. These will be covered in the following chapters:

- Takt Time
- Load levelling
- Theory of production pull
- Kanban systems
- Visual management
- Calculating requirements

1. Takt Time

To understand JIT you must first understand takt time. A common misunderstanding is the belief that takt time has a relationship to or actually is the production cycle time. This is not correct.

Takt time is actually determined from the demand from the customer in relation to the operating hours. In other words the required frequency of each completed part. An often missed component is the relationship to the operating hours or available production time. If the available production time is not an included parameter the flexibility required to achieve takt time will be missing.

So how does takt time differ from cycle time? Let's have a look at what cycle time is and how it is determined.

A production system is generally made up of many smaller processes and pieces of machinery / equipment. Each of these individual processes will have a cycle time that is determined by three main factors:

- Machine auto cycle time
- Manual cycle time
- Load and Unload time
- Changeover time

The process cycle time is the combined time of the above. The total cycle time is the sum of all process cycle times plus any waiting, transport and inventory time.

Now let's have a look at how takt time is calculated.

The most important point to make regarding takt time is that takt time has nothing to do with processing or cycle time. Takt time is often referred to as the 'beat of the customer'.

The formula to calculate takt time is:

T / D

Where:

T = Available Time

D = Customer Demand

Available time is calculated by taking the total operating time, less breaks and planned stoppages, less planned downtime. I like to calculate this based on a single day, however this can be calculated based on a week or month in situations with low demand or availability – more on this later.

For a single day calculation the following formula for available time is used:

Operating hours − total break time = 27360 (sec)

Parallel production streams (full production lines producing same part) = 2

Total planned downtime (includes both production lines) = 2700 (sec)

27360 x 2 - 2700 = 52020

In the above example the operating day is 8.5 hours and has an unpaid 30 minute lunch break and 24 minutes of other paid breaks throughout the day. This leaves an effective work day of 7.6 hours or 7 hours and 36 minutes. The facility has two productions lines producing the same part; these lines are independent of each other and share no machinery or process steps. There is also planned downtime of 45 minutes on one of the lines on this day.

Let's say the customer demand is 600 units per day for this example. When we apply the takt time formula from the previous page – 52020 / 600 – 86.7. Our takt time on this day is 87.6 seconds; this means a part needs to be completed every 87.6 seconds to keep up with customer demand. If we produce faster than this we will over produce and create inventory. Overproduction is the worst of the seven wastes as it contributes to all of the other wastes. If we produce slower than 87.6 seconds we will not meet the customers demand and will have to deploy overtime or rely on inventory produced earlier; both of these are wastes of sorts.

This is where the difference between takt time and cycle time is important to understand. The total or overall cycle time is technically irrelevant, what is important is the individual process cycle times in comparison to the takt time; this will be discussed in greater detail in the next chapter.

By concerning ourselves with and measuring performance against takt time we are thinking about the customers requirements; we are not constrained in our thinking by what we believe are the best possible cycle times. By focusing on meeting the customer demand we open opportunities for innovation and continuous improvement.

Because the takt time is calculated from the demand and the available time, the takt time can vary from day to day and can vary significantly throughout months and years. Both of the factors in the formula are variables. The production system needs to be flexible an agile enough to respond to changes in demand and available time (often due to planned / unplanned downtime). Steps and solutions to help achieve this flexibility are contained in the following pages and in other titles in the Your 60 Minute Lean Business series. Having a robust demand planning system is one solution that can be effective. This enables the production to be leveled across a period of time rather than relying solely on leveling production and workloads through the production process alone. Demand planning does have inherent risks of creating inventory if not effectively managed.

2. Load Leveling

The term load leveling can apply to many different aspects of business. In the context of this book we will be discussing load leveling on two fronts. The first will be analyzing takt time and cycle time with a view to balancing and the second will be machine and operator load leveling to eliminate overburden and underutilization. Separately these two areas of change can significantly improve your efficiencies; together they will have an even greater impact and enable you to meet your customer's requirements in a cost effective manner. Load leveling is often referred to as heijunka – this is a Japanese term and methodology which is used in Toyota Production System (TPS).

Takt Time vs Cycle Time

It is important to compare the cycle times of the machines used in your production streams against the required takt time. Just in time is all about eliminating the wastes of manufacturing, particularly over production as this will result in inventory, transportation, rework and possibly over processing; if you have machine cycle times that are greater than the takt time you will have to put in place solutions. This analysis will provide the information necessary to make informed decisions.

To simplify the explanation we'll use an example based on a fictional production line scenario. The parameters of the scenario are as follows:

Takt time – 94 seconds

Machine cycle times:

1. 44 seconds

2. 62 seconds

3. 65 seconds

4. 105 seconds

5. 57 seconds

6. 96 seconds

The first step has already been completed as we know the takt time and we have measured the machine cycle times. The next step is to chart the measurements.

By charting the results of the measurement analysis it can be clearly visualized which machines operate outside of the takt time. These are machines four and six. It is also clear the imbalance between the machines used in this process; the difference between the shortest and longest machine time is over double. This will make it difficult to balance the production line.

If all of the machines in the above example were to run at their capacity we would see a buildup of stock between machines 1 and 2, 2 and 3, 3 and 4 and 5 and 6. If this is a single piece flow production line we would have machine 5 waiting for the completion of machine 4 and due to machines 4 and 6 cycle times being greater than the takt time we would not meet customer demand.

So what are the options available to us to solve this problem? There are at least four options:

1) Produce finished product to the longest cycle time and fail to achieve takt time. This will result in a failure to supply the customer on time and could lead to a loss of sales.

2) Have all machines operating at capacity (cycle time). This will result in inventory as discussed in the above paragraph and will still result in a failure to supply the customer. Once again, this could lead to a loss of customers and sales.

3) Kaizen the machinery to reduce the variance in cycle times across the line. This can achieve some improvement, however with the variance so great between M/C 1 and M/C 4 this approach is likely to prove challenging and probably quite expensive.

4) Build stock of finished product ahead of schedule. This will enable supply to customer demand when stock levels are managed, however will result in higher inventory levels which in turn can lead to rework. It is likely that cash flow would also be impacted by this practice.

5) Build to kanban (discussed in chapter 4) or determined stock levels for each step. This will eliminate or reduce the impacts of the issues identified in option 4; however customer demand will not be met unless some machine kaizen is successfully undertaken on machines 4 and 6.

OPERATOR LOAD LEVELLING

This is similar to the above discussion, however we are focusing now on operators rather than machines. There are two reasons for us to analyse the operator loads.

1) To ensure takt time can be achieved

2) To ensure operator workloads are equalized to avoid overburden and / or underutilisation.

The problems with overburdening operators are many and include:

- Increased likelihood of OHS issues arising; this is both from overuse injury and hazards / injuries caused by fatigue.
- Increased likelihood of poor quality resulting from fatigue and / or rushing through the workload

- Poor productivity

Problems arising from underutilisation are similar in result with increased likelihood of OHS issues and quality problems. In the case of underutilisation however these are caused by inactivity which reduces a persons awareness.

Uneven workloads can lead to morale issues amongst the work teams. Poor morale is one on the great negative forces in any business. Morale is not only a good indicator of an organisations management; it is also a barrier to success or a precursor to failure.

The best tool to balance the operator workload is through standardised work. Your 60 Minute Lean Business – Standardised Work is available in paperback and ebook.

YAMAZUMI CHART

A Yamazumi chart is a stacked chart used to show the steps within a process and the breakdown of work type. These work types are Value Adding, Incidental and Waste. As the objective of lean is to identify and eliminate waste in the value stream, a Yamazumi chart is a valuable tool.

The above example shows how a Yamazumi chart breaks down the three work types. It is clearly shown in the example that value added work makes up less than a third of the total cycle time. A standard spreadsheet application can be used to develop the charts.

3. Theory of Pull Production

Before discussing pull production, let's look at the traditional push method of production flow.

Push Production

With traditional push production flow the product is "pushed" through the production process. If we look at a general manufacturing business the following high level flow may occur:

1) Sales order received

2) Job planned for manufacture

3) Materials purchased

4) Production scheduled

5) Materials received

6) Materials into inventory

7) Production schedule received by production

8) Raw materials enter production

9) First processing step completed

10) Part finished product to inventory or waiting

11) Second process step scheduled

12) Parts collected / delivered to second process step

13) Second process step completed

14) Finished part into inventory

15) Sales order opened

16) Picking slip raised

17) Product picked

18) Product invoiced

19) Product shipped to customer

The above is a very simple two process manufacturing value stream and look at how many steps are involved. Also note there are four inventory steps. Whenever we have inventory, we add cost, risk safety and quality and impact efficiency.

If we were to develop a current state value stream map of such a model we would see something similar to the below diagram. Note the high amount of non-value added time in inventory and the high dependency on Planning to co-ordinate the pulling of product from inventory and processing. Just over one percent of the lead time is actually processing time; the balance is waiting in inventory in this example. Many businesses are not much better placed than this believe it or not.

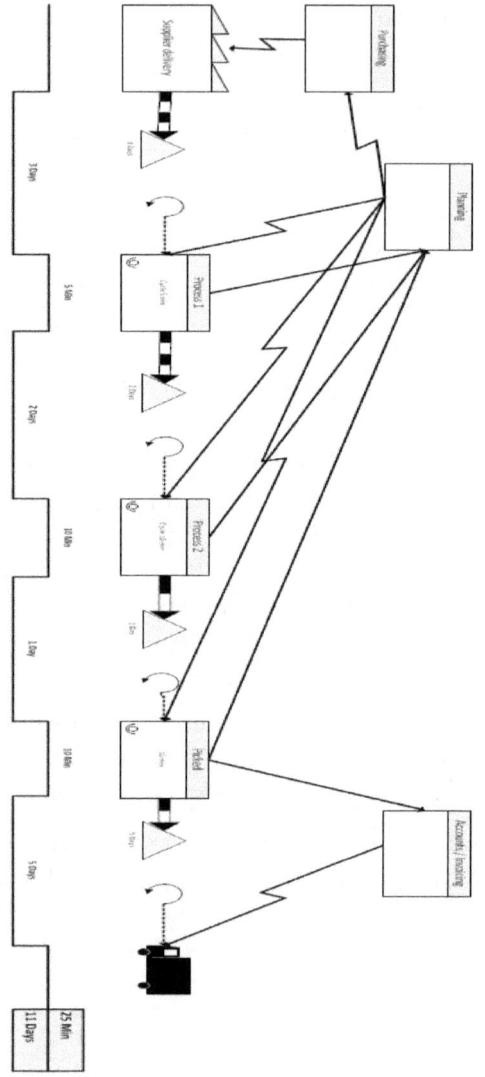

The below diagram illustrates how a conventional push production system operates. Notice the involvement of planning all through the production process. This involvement may by large or small, however it is always present when a push method is practiced.

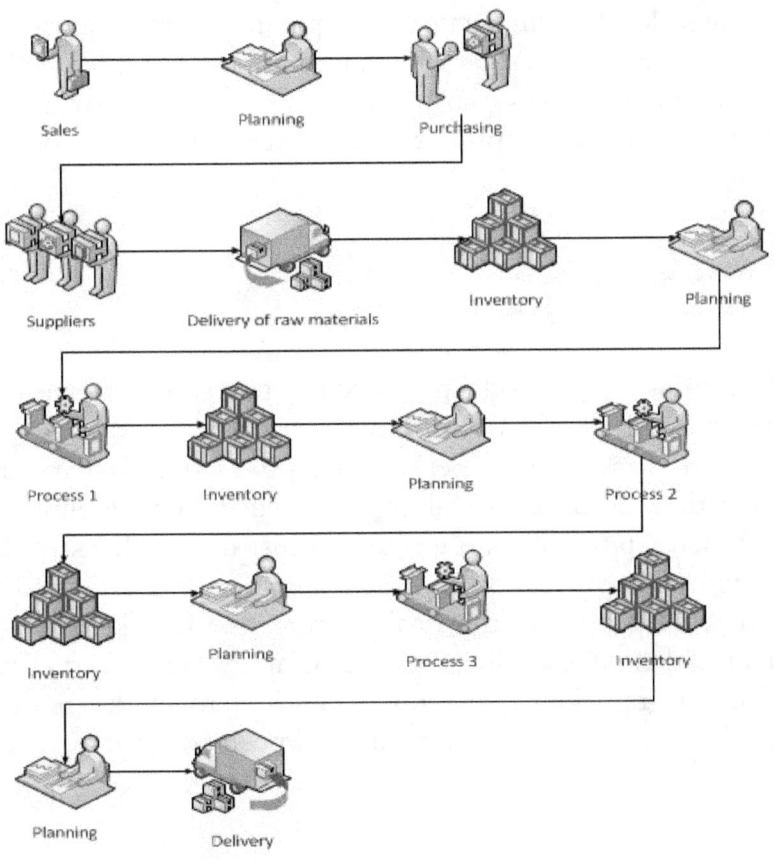

As you can see from the above illustration of a simple three stage manufacturing business, the processes can become quite long winded and very dependent on support services.

For example, planning is involved five times in the above example. There are also four inventory stages; every time we have inventory, we are tying up capital.

To summarise the push method, we have a lot of inventory, waiting and interaction with planning/production control. The high level of interaction with planning and production control may not seem too big an issue however every time this interaction takes place resources are taken away from adding value to the product. Any excessive interaction is waste.

Pull Production

By contrast, pull production occurs almost in reverse by principle. Rather than the primary instruction going to the first process step, in a perfect pull production system, an instruction to dispatch will be provided to the warehouse. This instruction will start a series of instructions backwards through the process flow. The warehouse will request a completed part from the final process step or take from a supermarket which will trigger the completion of a part. The below diagram illustrates how a pull system works; notice the differences from the conventional push system.

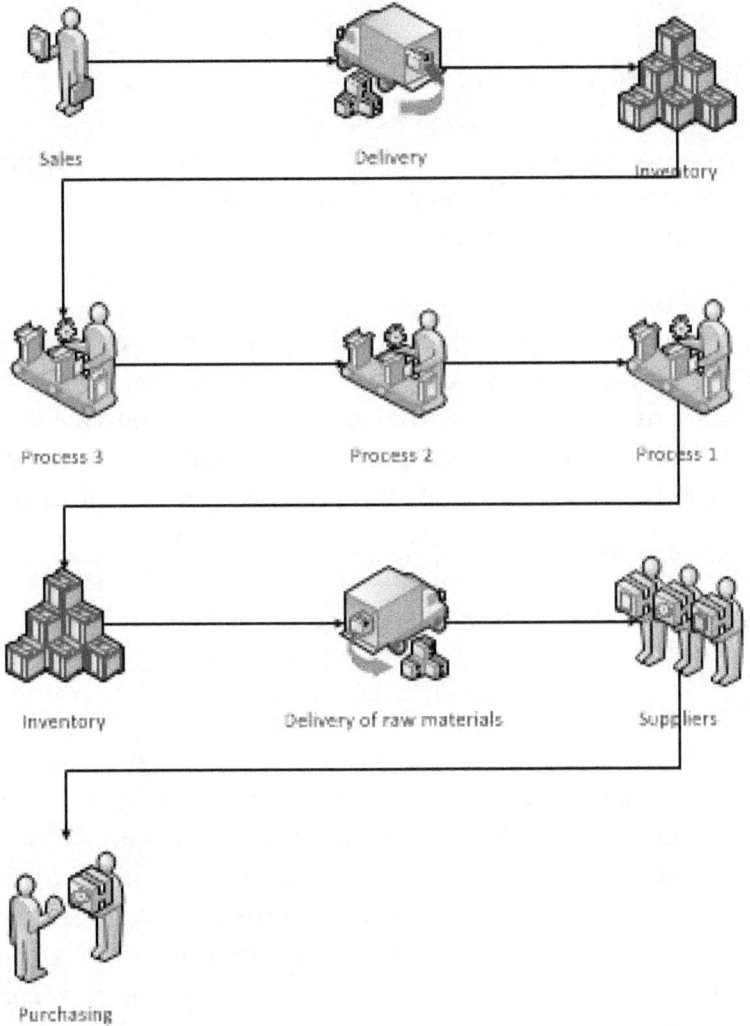

As you can see, the primary instruction to manufacture is to the final manufacturing process. There are a number of keys to an effective pull production system. Kanban is the trigger system used to initiate production at each step and is discussed in detail in the next chapter; visual management is used to clearly communicate the status of the systems and is discussed in Chapter 5; a leveled production process and matched inventory system are also keys. Leveled production was discussed in Chapter 2, now we will begin to understand why it is important.

The major keys to an effective pull production system are defining where in the process to hold inventory to maximize JIT and minimize cost of inventory and how much inventory to carry. Even a perfect one piece flow system requires some inventory of components. As we all know inventory is one the seven wastes; therefore we require any inventory to be measured and managed. Every business, product and system is unique so a flat rule cannot be given, however there are some guidelines that can be used.

> 1) At what points in the production process does the raw material become a "product"? In every process there is a point where we go from stocking components to assemblies, this point in the process is important to identify. Some organisations setup their bills of material at these point to call them sub-assemblies or "child parts". It is often at these points that supermarkets can be setup. It is also at these points that the sub-assemblies may be commonly used in a variety of assemblies or "parent parts". Thus providing more than one single demand point for the sub-assemblies in the supermarket

2) How many parent parts create demand for the sub-assemblies? The greater the number of parent parts creating demand reduces the risk of dead inventory.

3) What is the averaged, peak and low demand for the sub-assembly? If demand is not constant or stable for this subassembly then a supermarket may create more waste (inventory).

4) What is the total processing time to manufacture to the sub-assembly stage? If the processing time to this stage is greater than takt time then extra shifts or other alternatives may be required with a supermarket setup to hold inventory.

5) Is the production line used for any other products or is it stand alone? If a line is multipurpose, the availability of resources (man and machine) will be limited compared to a standalone line where the manpower can be utilized elsewhere and the machinery left idle.

The below VSM diagram shows the same process used in the push production example, however now in a pull production method. Note, there has been no kaizen or standardized work applied so the cycle times and inventory are the same.

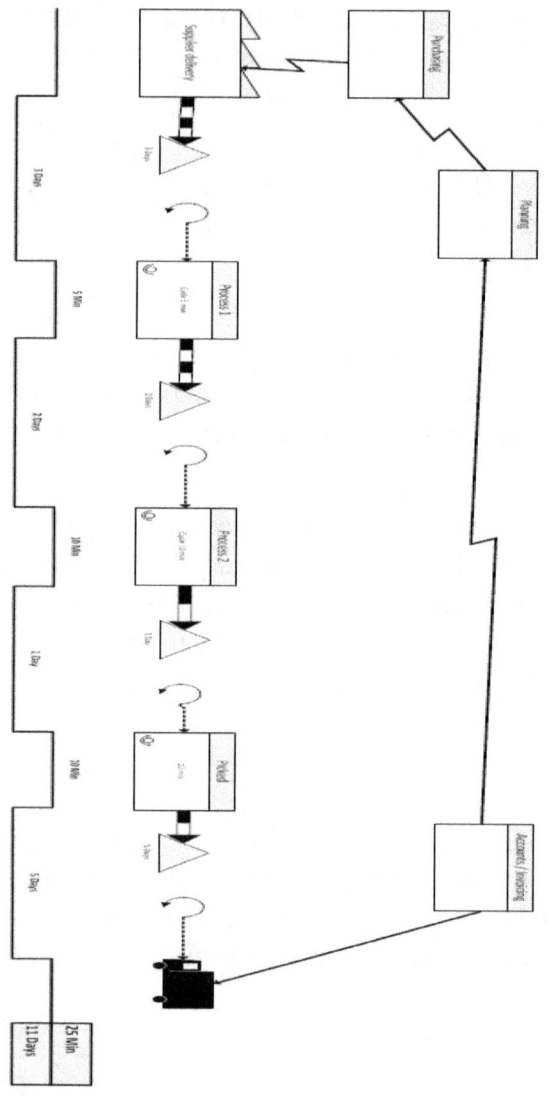

As you can see, even without improvements to the processes, the communication has been greatly reduced by implementing a Pull Methodology. Alone, this reduction in communication requirements will:

- Reduce resource requirements for administration

- Reduce / eliminate errors brought about by incorrect communications

The true benefits of pull production are realised through the reduction of inventory throughout the processing. Because each process step is producing to the demand of the next step (or supermarket requirement; it must be said here that a supermarket doesn't have to hold a large inventory, it can hold a single item) overproduction will not occur. To manage a pull production system, there needs to be a trigger to produce at each step; the best system to manage this is through the use of kanban.

4. Kanban

The term kanban comes directly from the Toyota Production System and literally means 'board'. Often, kanban is incorrectly described as a material management system; kanban is simply a system used to trigger an activity (this could be production, material movement or shipment).

Kanban can take many different forms, however the most common is a card system which will be used for the following explanation before providing details of some other common systems.

Kanban Card

The simple kanban card is probably the most common type of kanban used. The card can take many forms, however usually contains the following information:

- Part / Inventory Number
- Part / Inventory Name
- Short description
- Image of component
- Kanban type
- Supplier
- Qty on Kanban

- Lead time
- Item location
- Card / Kanban Number of
- Responsible planner / buyer

The Kanban system is a replenishment system used in place of a materials requirement planning (MRP) system. The two systems are not intended to be used for the same parts. This is where many businesses come unstuck; they use a kanban system and continue to use their MRP system. This creates confusion and / or complacency. A card system works by triggering the supplier (this can be internal or external) to produce a part or quantity of parts. It really can be that simple. Some businesses choose to maintain an internal only kanban system; in these instances the trigger is often used to initiate the purchasing process from a supplier. While not as effective in reducing waste as a supplier kanban, this model can still provide good benefits.

A simple internal kanban process between a warehouse and production is defined in the following diagram.

The kanban is triggered by the shipment of a part to the customer. In classic pull production theory this action creates demand on production to produce a part. The kanban card is returned to production as a trigger to fill the demand. When the part is completed it is returned to the warehouse with the kanban card. The colour-coding is used to visually display the urgency. When the first card is returned to production both the warehouse staff and production staff can easily see there is a demand, however as there is still stock available in the warehouse (in this case two) the replacement can be made with normal priority. If the second card is returned to production it is clear there is now some urgency as stock is now low. When the third card is returned to production, the warehouse is now out of stock and replacements should be expedited. There is some science behind the volumes which will be explained in further detail in a later section.

In the above example, two simple three position kanban boards are used – one in the warehouse and another in production. A single card is stored in each position meaning the inventory of finished goods will not exceed three units. For a low volume selling item this may be okay, for larger volume items there are a couple of options.

1) Increase the number of pegs and cards to increase the total size of inventory.

2) Store multiple cards on each peg. Once again this will increase the total size of inventory.

Of these two options the first offers greater visibility and control of inventory. A simple system as above can be effective for high or low volume parts and can be used throughout the value stream to trigger staged production, materials, and even resource planning. Kanban will work in small, medium or large organisations and can be effectively implemented without expensive infrastructure or technology.

A card kanban system does require resources to monitor and collect cards; this is often tasked to material handlers on a material route. It is also important to highlight the need to manage the kanban system. Just like any other system there is an element of management and maintenance required for the system to consistently operate at its optimum level. This maintenance may be required for a number of reasons including:

 - Changes in demand

 - Changes in design or specification

 - Changes in supplier

- Lost or damaged cards

Bin System Kanban

Another common type of Kanban system is the Bin System. While the concept of a trigger is the same as with the Kanban card, a bin system is used in place of the cards and visual boards. There are two main variations to the Bin System; Two Bin and Three Bin.

Two Bin System

As the name implies this is a system comprising of two bins; one at the user and the other in the process of replenishment. A two bin system can be useful where demand is low and parts are complex so a minimum level of inventory provides significant cost benefits.

Three Bin System

Similar to the two bin system, this system utilizes three bins and is the more common of the bin type Kanban systems in use. Once again, one bin will be at the user, one at the supplier being replenished and in this instance the third will be in transit to the user or in transit to the supplier. The benefit of this system over the two bin system is the faster replenishment to the user when the replenishment is triggered. Whereas the two bin system where the trigger to replenish comes when the first bin is empty or returned creating a gap in supply as the full bin from the supplier is transported, the third bin is constantly in transit or awaiting internal movement to the work area. This does increase the total inventory or WIP within the system as there are now three bins rather than two.

Although there are some different methods to manage the replenishment the basics of kanban remain. A signal is used to trigger the replenishment method. Whether you use the cards and visual board, a bin system, a combination or any other method the basic principles are the same.

Many organizations struggle through the implementation of kanban due to a misconception that once implemented, a kanban system no longer requires management. Just like any other system, it will require monitoring, measurement and management as discussed earlier. This is an important concept to understand; resources must be made available. Another reason businesses struggle is the lack of planning and understanding of the system setup.

Kanban System Setup

For any system there are certain requirements that will ensure the optimum results. With kanban these requirements are largely the calculations as discussed below.

As in everything else, there are almost as many formulae for kanban calculations as there are lines of inventory. I am a believer in keeping things simple, so with this approach I give you the simple kanban calculation.

$$\frac{\text{Daily Demand} \times \text{Lead Time (Days)} \times \text{Safety Factor}}{\text{Container Size}}$$

Daily demand is simply the average daily usage of the part. If you use the item sporadically, take a total over a month or even quarter and divide by the number of days to determine the daily demand.

Lead time is the time taken for delivery (from either internal or external supplier) from the day the kanban is triggered until physical parts are available on line for use. This is measured in days to enable easy calculation with daily demand.

The safety factor is a measure of your confidence in your systems, processes and suppliers. The standard is 1; if you have very low confidence this may be a 2. In between 1 and 2 provides the levels of confidence.

Container size is the number of parts in each container. This may be 1 or as high as you like. This enables you to talk in containers rather than total quantity of parts.

To give the formula some substance here it is again with some data around it:

Daily Demand = 25 units
Lead Time = 5 days
Safety Factor = 1
Container Size = 25

For the above data, the formula would look like this:

$$\frac{25 \times 5 \times 1}{25}$$

The result would be 5 containers or 125 units. This is the total amount of parts within the kanban system for this particular part. Where these are situated within the system is negotiated between you and the supplier. They will be either;

1) In your store

2) At your supplier

3) In transit

4) At a 3rd party

We can change the data used to make in more interesting:

Daily Demand = 30 units
Lead Time = 3 days
Safety Factor = 1.4
Container size = 15

$$\frac{30 \times 3 \times 1.4}{15}$$

This results in 8.4 containers or 126 units; we will round-up the containers to the next whole one. Never round-down! This will result in 9 containers or 135 units in the system. As we work with the supplier and gain more confidence in their performance the safety factor can reduce which will result in a reduction of the total quantity to a minimum of 6 containers or 90 units (3 days inventory). Remember, this inventory is not all within your system as roughly 1/3 will be in process with your supplier, 1/3 in transit and 1/3 in stock.

I have intentionally used a simple formula to both aide comprehension and simplify the explanations. I use the same formula in every business I work with and have for more than ten years. There are many more complex formulae used by many practitioners and I'm sure some do have some benefits however in my experience the more complex the system, the more problems will be met along your journey.

A kanban system should be easy to use, easy to determine when it is working on track and even easier to determine when it is off track! That is the beauty of kanban, you shouldn't need a PhD to setup the system or use the system. An effective system can be setup and managed by just about anyone and everyone in the business should be able to determine whether there is a problem or not.

After setting up and running your kanban system you may find there are some issues with either excess inventory or out of stock. Don't panic and throw out the system. This just means your calculations are a little (or a lot) off. As you gain experience in setting up kanban systems you will reduce these errors; remember though, the kanban system isn't a set and leave system. It is a dynamic system that will require updates in line with demand, product changes and supplier performance.

5. Visual Management

Visual management is a very general term and plays a significant role in lean organisations. In this chapter, we will discuss firstly visual management in general, followed by visual management specifically for JIT management.

General Visual Management

Visual management is all around us. We see it in the supermarkets, when driving, when watching television. In today's society it really is everywhere. How do you know where to purchase the fuel for your car? Visual management! All of the service stations display their prices and the benefits of making your purchase with them; you select the one that best suits your needs. This is visual management.

When embarking on a flying holiday, how do you know where to find the airport? Visual management!

Have you ever noticed how difficult some cities are to navigate? The easier ones have clear relevant signage that don't rely on words alone. Once again this is visual management.

I think you get the message; visual management is all around us, in all parts of our life. The key to effective visual management is to clearly communicate with as little complexity as possible.

Let's look at some examples of general visual management.

1) The below sign is so simple. It contains both words in English and a universal symbol meaning do not enter.

2) Another classic simple sign. This time First Aid.

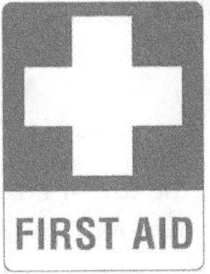

3) Once again we have symbols to assist in the comprehension of these common signs. Note the use of colours – red to denote prohibited.

4) The No Smoking sign doesn't even use words to get its point across.

In all of the above examples, the use of images or symbols helps the sharing of the information. In none of these instances do the communicators rely on words alone to get their message across. Very simple strategy; the challenge is to make this work for other types of communication.

Now let's discuss some visual management used in some other areas. The world of marketing is often overlooked when discussing effective visual management, I believe they provide some valuable lessons. What are the most recognizable images I around the globe? MacDonald's and Coca-Cola; all around the world when these logos are displayed most of the population will know exactly what they are. Yes, they are marketed extensively and effectively however it is nothing more than very effective visual management.

Visual Management in the workplace

In the business environment, visual management is used to communicate many things including:

- OHS information
- Company policies
- General communications
- 5S storyboards and audit boards
- Standardized work instructions

The list really does go on and on, one of the best uses of visual management is for Just in Time and especially kanban.

For JIT, visual management can be used to communicate the standard work used to control the materials handling. Just like for a manufacturing or office process where standardized work is used, it should be used for the delivery and distribution of the materials. This standardized work will include the material handler's route, frequency and inventory count and will be tied in with the process standardized work and takt time. This visual management can be in the form of central boards or displays and / or on the material handling trolley (if in use). If displayed centrally, this will have two benefits:

1) The material handler/s will have a backup location for their route and timings.

2) The work of the material handler/s will be openly distributed and communicated. This will result in easy auditing of the work and a broad understanding of the route. This will reduce the amount of chasing up by other departments.

Visual management in the warehouse for JIT can be as simple as labelling of racking, locations and inventory to min/max levels, restocking timings and Kanban boards. It can also be used in a similar way for line-side stocking where a conventional warehouse is not used or is the supplier to the line-side primary locations.

We discussed the Kanban Board earlier in this book, the kanban board is a form of visual management. Kanban is often linked closely with a manufacturing or warehousing environment as this is where the concept originated. Many people don't realize kanban can be used just as effectively in the office, service and IT environments. As the name kanban mean "trigger" it can be used to trigger any activity; kanban is a perfect system to use for project management. This use of visual management is still JIT as we are using the visual management to trigger the next steps of a business process.

6. Pulling it all together

So far we have looked at the theories of takt time; load levelling; pull production; Kanban and visual management. Now let's look at how all of this comes together to give us a Just in Time system. The best way to explain how this all works is to work backwards through what we have learnt so far.

In the context of JIT, visual management is the method used to communicate the process and the status of the process. It is also used to train, audit and review the process. Without visual management would the JIT system still work? In some instances it would still work however it never will be as effective. To say visual management is just the communication of the system is selling it a fair bit short as it is an integrated part of a sustainable system.

Kanban is a control method, just as many organisations use a Materials Resource Planning (MRP) system, others use Kanban to control the ordering, supply and distribution of materials, part finished and finished product. Some organisations even try a combination of MRP and kanban with varying results. As neither of these systems are developed to be run with the other it can be challenging to get good results from this combined method. I have seen a couple of organisations pull it off with some success however I'm not convinced this is the right approach due to the amount of controls and management required to ensure both systems are running in alignment. A better approach is to use the kanban system to manage the supply, delivery and distribution and use the accounting side of the MRP system only to capture and record the transactions. While the best MRP systems can be effective in managing the supply chain, an easy and effective kanban system will reduce the amount of system support and system management required.

While kanban is a method used to control a JIT system, pull production is at the heart of JIT. Pull production is both the driving force and the end result of a JIT system. With a pull production system you are reversing the traditional ideas of batch processing. Understanding the concept of pull production is absolutely critical to the success of a JIT system. With the traditional push method of production, each process produces as fast as it can and builds up stock at the output side of the process. This stock is transported to either inventory or the next process step when scheduled. Each process produces independent of the other processes with little or no consideration of inventory levels other than the scheduling or planning system. With a push system you are relying heavily on the scheduling and planning to be of a high standard; this does make the production system less nimble to changes as the lead times can be longer. In contrast, a JIT system can be more nimble due to the reduced inventory levels and reduced involvement required from scheduling and planning. A pull system empowers the production team to reduce inventory levels and achieve greater true efficiency through production of customer requirements only (not making to stock).

Whereas the last three stages are the process, controls and communication, load levelling is one of the requirements of a JIT system. This is because for a JIT system to be effective and sustainable it is important to have the material flowing efficiently through the processes with little or no impact by bottlenecks. To achieve this, the line must be balanced, otherwise the bottlenecks will stop the flow and create pockets of high and low inventory. Whenever inventory pockets show up they must be managed; this can be achieved through a supermarket to feed a process after a low inventory process or to capture before a bottleneck. Supermarkets are a commonly used control when line balancing cannot be achieved. It needs to be understood though, that whenever a supermarket is used your inventory levels are increasing and this will impact cashflow as well as introduce the risks associated with over-production. These risks include:

- Rework or scrap due to changes in design or obsoletion

- Excessive transportation and movement of stock

- Safety risks associated with the above

The challenge is to identify the opportunities to level the load without falling into the trap of too many supermarkets. The supermarket is an easy option, however should be used as the last resort or when the return on investment in the quest for levelling cannot be justified.

This brings us to takt time, the heartbeat of the customer. Without understanding the takt time the next steps would be impossible to do effectively. Remember, takt time is simply the available work time divided by the customer demand and tells you the required frequency for finished product. Understanding takt time is the key to your sustainable success with a JIT supply chain and broader lean business system.

7. Some more tools

This chapter contains a couple of useful tools that can be used to assist a business in achieving and maintaining an effective JIT system. The tools in this section are not prerequisites or 'must haves', however can be of great benefit and assistance in the overall lean system.

Tool 1) Quick change over

Quick change over (QCO) has a couple of alternative names:

- Quick Die Change Over (QDCO)
- Single Minute Exchange of Dies (SMED)

The reason I have removed the reference to Dies in the title is to maintain a relevance in the greater business environment. In today's world, most businesses do not use dies in their process; even if they are in manufacturing. Just because a business doesn't use dies doesn't mean they don't have change overs. Even in an office or administration environment there are changeover processes that occur. The ability to changeover in a shorter amount of time than a competitor can save you money and give you a genuine competitive advantage in the market. How do you calculate your changeover time?

The total time from last completed (good) part to the completion of the next completed (good) part is defined as the changeover time. A good part is defined as a usable part that meets the correct specifications and can be a manufactured part, an engineered part or even a document. The changeover time is broken down into two parts:

- External time / elements
- Internal time / elements

External time consists work elements that can be performed while the last part and / or first part are being produced. External components can only be achieved where there are automated processes within the work elements (not changeover elements) or by another operator / resource. With automated processes the operator is free to prepare for, begin or complete the changeover process while the last and / or first parts are being produced.

Internal time consists of all work elements that are performed while no parts are being produced. This is similar in definition to incidental work time in that the internal changeover work elements must be performed to enable production to commence, however the time taken to perform these functions takes away from the value adding time.

The target of QCO is to reduce (or as much as possible eliminate) the internal time / elements of the changeover to increase the value add time. This is done by following the

Standardized Work methodology however instead of measuring and improving the processing elements you are measuring the elements of the changeover. A more thorough instruction can be found in the book 'Your 60 Minute Lean Business – Standardized Work'; but here is a quick overview of how to implement the Standardized Work method for changeovers:

1) First measure the entire changeover time from last good part to first good part. If possible measure multiple changeovers to understand the repeatable time and any common issues identified across the multiple examples.

2) Measure the changeover again, this time taking note of the element steps of the changeover. Make sure you record whether the steps are internal or external. Once again, multiple recordings are recommended wherever possible.

3) Calculate the total internal and external time separately, to indicate where the waste in the process is contained.

4) Analyse the internal changeover elements. These should be reduced or eliminated first as these elements are performed when the process has stopped and is true waste. Remember the customer only pays for the value added processes.

5) When the internal element improvements have been exhausted (at least those prioritized with good return on investment or ROI) you can analyze the external elements to identify opportunities. Improvements in the external elements will not achieve a reduction in overall changeover time or waste, however can result in other efficiency gains by freeing up labour resources for other activities.

By reducing the changeover times in your business you can achieve greater line balancing and reduce the requirement for inventory between processing steps and achieve improved JIT performance.

Dedicated material handlers

An area many businesses fail to resource in the drive toward a lean business is that of materials handling. Unfortunately many quickly forget the real objective of lean and simply (and incorrectly) believe lean is 'doing more with less'. This approach can lead to failure. Lean is about doing more with the right resources. Under resourcing can lead to just as much waste as over resourcing. Effective material handling resources are imperative to achieving a sustainable and effective JIT system. So how do you know if you have the right amount of resources?

First, we need to look at what these resources might be. Obviously, a business can employ manual handlers to undertake the material movement throughout the business. Many businesses utilize technology for the material handling and with the costs and associated management systems of robotics becoming less and less this is becoming more accessible to a broader type of business. This technology can be as simple as conveyors to as hi-tech as automated robots delivering on a standardized route.

Once you have determined the type of material handling resources it is necessary to determine the resource requirements. This must come after the JIT standardized work has been defined as these calculations will determine the number of resources. Just as we work to balance the work on a production line, we should work to balance the load for the material handlers. A simple Yamazumi chart measured against takt time will enable these calculations to be effective.

Your 60 Minute Lean Business

Jidoka / Quality

Contents

Title	Page
What is Jidoka?	3
1. Andon	6
2. Pokayoke	9
3. Statistical Analysis	17
4. PPAP	28
5. Standards	33
6. Documentation	38

What is Jidoka

Put very simply, Jidoka means "automation with a human element". This is the Toyota definition and is highly focused on an automated production line process. The four elements of jidoka are:

1) Detection of a problem
2) Stop the line
3) Correct the immediate problem
4) Conduct root cause analysis and develop / implement corrective action to eliminate recurrence

Although developed for an automated line, the same elements of jidoka are just as effective in any environment and can even be effective in an office or service environment. The examples contained within this book will be focused on a manufacturing environment, however some examples will be used in other business types to show the versatility of jidoka. There are a number of tools used in the delivery of jidoka; the most common two are poka yoke and andon – these will be explained in detail in later chapters.

In addition to the specific tools of jidoka there is also the cultural aspects. This is the empowerment of all employees to stop production when a problem is identified. This may not sound like much, but when you think about it further and you understand the training and coaching that has gone into the employees to develop every one of them to the point where management trusts them all to make the decision to stop production you begin to understand why this is such a powerful culture.

Jidoka is one of the pillars of the Lean Business System as is shown in the Lean House diagram below.

Lean Business

Jidoka – Quality		Just In Time
	Standardised Work	**Kaizen**
	5S	**TPM**

A direct outcome from the jidoka culture and practice is an improvement in product quality. This is why the two are linked in the above diagram. Many practitioners have determined the two are synonymous. I believe there is a distinct difference between the two in the approach and the reasons for their use however when used together the benefits can be significantly greater than when used independently.

In this book I have separated the two, with jidoka and the direct tools being discussed in the earlier chapters and quality systems and formal certification being discussed in the later chapters.

1. Andon

The Japanese word andon doesn't directly translate into English, however the andon is the name of the traditional paper lanterns seen in Japan (more so historically). In the context of jidoka, the andon is traditionally a light signaling a problem or a line stoppage. The most common method of triggering the light is the andon cord.

The andon cord is a cord usually hung above and along a production line. The cord is similar to the old fashioned cords in trams and trains used to request the driver to stop – some were also used to apply the brakes. So it isn't a new idea – like most of the concepts within lean.

When an operator identifies a problem on the production line they pull the cord to alert the production supervisor – in some instances the cord also stops the line, just like the old trains. Not all systems allow the operator to stop the line, however those organisations with the better and trusting cultures do allow the operators to stop the line.

When the cord is pulled, a light system and/or siren is triggered to alert the supervisor, some systems have an escalation process built in to alert management on subsequent pulls of the cord. If the system allows, the line is stopped to enable the immediate problem to be corrected. The team (this may include Production Operators, Management, Engineering, Maintenance, Quality representatives) determine whether the line can be restarted or if other corrective work is required before the line is returned to normal operation.

Once the line is restarted, the team will then determine the cause of the problem through one of the root cause analysis tools. Once the root cause has been determined, the team then defines what corrective actions are required to eliminate the problem from recurring. Once again, this team could be diverse and is usually predetermined based on the problem type.

Similar systems operate in many businesses across many industries. For instance, in retail establishments, the checkout operator may have a button they press to alert the supervisor that assistance is required.

In a hospital, the patient can press a button on their bed to alert the nursing staff; hospitals have automated this in many areas now so when a patient is in distress, the alert is automated through an alarm system to the nursing station and the relevant medical team.

So why give the operators the power to stop production? When you empower the entire team to make that call you are creating a quality culture; when something isn't right management can trust the team to make the decision to get it right. Of course, there is a lot of training that goes into the team members to get them to the point where the correct decisions are made. The training is well worth it though.

What level of training is required? Before you go about training you have to set the standards of quality that are expected – this expectation must be agreed and communicated across the business and to the market. This is an important step; many businesses try to improve product quality without setting or communicating a standard. Once the standards have been set and communicated you can go about the training. The training program needs to be designed to achieve the safety, product quality, throughput / efficiency standards and should be presented by an experienced operator and trainer; it isn't good enough to employ a smooth presenter if they do not have the practical experience.

If you choose to empower the staff to stop the line without this level of training you will likely encounter chaos in the production system as the line stoppages are likely to be too frequent and randomly caused. This will result in one of a couple of outcomes:

1) The andon and possibly the lean journey may be challenged or possibly even fail as a result of the chaos created.

2) The chaos may result in a financial loss to the organisation as the relatively uncontrolled stoppages cause delays in production.

3) Possibly the worst outcome is if the new chaos becomes the 'business as usual' and could have long term and far reaching business implications.

This chaos can sometimes be used as a trigger event (I have been guilty of doing this in the past) and can be an effective method when used once. If it's required more than the one time then you have cultural problems that need to be addressed. This is evident in organisations that are relying on a single point (person) to effect the culture change and to drive the improvements.

Why do we use andon? It is much less expensive and has far less impact on the customer when identified problems are fixed when they are identified rather than at the end of the production process. Every time a product is reworked late in the process the likelihood of extra rework (incidental rework) being required are greater. This all adds time and money to the process and can have an impact on delivery on time. When the problem is identified and the process stopped early, the schedule can be adjusted if necessary at that time. It is still possible to make up time in later processing steps to bring the job back on schedule; or you can discuss the potential late delivery with the customer at this time rather than on or after the due date.

Another benefit of andon is the problem is fixed where it is identified. This is generally means the right people are present for rectification, root cause analysis and learning. When inspection and rework is conducted post production you will have to either employ a specialist rework team or drag the resources away from the production processes to perform the rework; this will result in the line stopping anyway. When a specialist team perform the rework the learning does not easily find its way back to the production team.

2. Pokayoke

Pokayoke is a method of error proofing a process to eliminate the potential for errors or defects to pass through. Like many of the lean terms, pokayoke originated from the Toyota Production System, however the concept has been around for a long time prior to TPS. What Toyota did was to put a name and a methodology around the concept. I have a belief that no employee comes to work to do a bad job; it is up to the organisations management to help the employees do the best they can. This is where pokayoke comes in.

The operators shouldn't have to think too hard about the process when they are undertaking their tasks; the process should be easily followed and should be stable to produce repeatable outputs from efficiency to quality. To assist with this repeatability we incorporate pokayoke into our process design.

Rules of pokayoke

- Pokayoke must be built into the process; it should not be additional work; inspection is not pokayoke.

- Should be cost effective design - perform cost/ benefit analysis

- Should be simple design – don't introduce more complexity into the process

- Should control a real problem – introduce pokayoke where a problem exists or where analysis shows a high risk

- Must not hinder the operator or add health or safety risks to the process

The classis pokayoke story told is the production line where the problem was empty boxes being shipped to the customer. After many hours and dollars spent designing complicated and complex processes and engineered solutions to control the problem with mostly no success a simple addition of a fan at the end of the conveyor to blow the empty boxes off the line was installed with a high level of success. Now I don't know how true this story is; I'm sure somewhere this has been used as a pokeyoke and I have seen firsthand the use of compressed air to remove empty packaging from a production line. This is a very simple example.

The original Toyota pokayoke goes back to before they were an automotive powerhouse. Originally, Toyota manufactured looms. A regular problem was the thread would break and the machine would continue to produce defective material. The solution was to design a pokayoke into the machine to stop the processing when a thread broke. This reduced the wastage, increased production and heralded the revolution of methodical error proofing.

Design

The objective of a pokayoke is to eliminate the potential errors or defects and to best realize this is to engineer the problem out of the design. This can be achieved by following the principles of Design for Manufacture. This involves the entire organisation becoming engaged in the design stages through a collaborative approach. A strong understanding and recognition of the operational strengths and weaknesses is required to achieve effective design for manufacture. This can be developed through the use of a SWOT analysis.

SWOT

A SWOT analysis is a review of a business's strengths, weaknesses, opportunities and threats and is best performed by a cross functional team. It is best to begin with the strengths (as these are often better understood) and list out the identified strengths of the operations team. This is followed by the weaknesses; it is easy to simply list antonyms of the strengths when identifying the weaknesses, however you will achieve better results if you go deeper and identify real weaknesses.

Once the strengths and weaknesses have been defined, the next step is to list the opportunities; these may be extensions of your current strengths or capabilities. The final step is to define the threats; these are areas of risk and may be extensions of your weaknesses.

A good way to look at the SWOT is to think of strengths and weaknesses as internally controlled and the opportunities and threats as externally influenced.

Once the SWOT has been developed, it should be maintained at least annually as part of your business planning process (much more on this in another book). The effective use of this information will guide the design process to ensure that what is designed is within your operational capabilities. This is not to say you shouldn't stretch your capabilities and improve your manufacturing techniques however this should be done in a methodical and deliberate way.

Further than designing for manufacture, your designs should make errors in assembly not possible or at least very obvious. This can be achieved by designing parts identical or obviously different depending on the requirements. For example you can design left and right brackets symmetrical to remove the possibility of using the incorrect part or where this is not possible design them different so that the incorrect part cannot be used. These philosophies will not only remove the risk of errors they can also save you money by reducing the number of unique parts used in your designs and therefore reduce your overall inventory.

Where designing the errors away is not possible, the focus should shift to designing a mechanism within the process to error proof the process. The classic fan design described earlier is one approach and the designs really are limitless.

In a manufacturing business jig design can be an effective method of applying pokayoke. Mechanisms can be implemented to:

- Stop incorrect parts being assembled

- Control of dimensions

- Eliminate the requirement for inspection of critical characteristics

Pokayoke can be applied to other parts of the business or other business types. In a retail environment you can control the amount of shelf inventory by setting up the shelving to hold up to the maximum level; this is especially effective in the fresh produce and spoilable stock.

Another form of pokayoke that can be seen in the real world is the slot in the post box. This slot is dimensioned to receive standard letters only, ensuring oversized letters are posted via the counter where the correct postage costs can be charged. Even the shape sorter we all played with as kids is a form of pokayoke.

A simple rule of pokayoke is that it must absolutely control the risk and eliminate the error. Anything less than this is not really pokayoke but is more of a reduction of risk. Don't get me wrong, any reduction in the risk of errors occurring is a good thing; a better thing is error proofing.

So how do you go about designing a process pokayoke? There are a few simple rules that when followed will help ensure the errors are eliminated and the process design doesn't add more waste or other risks.

1) Genchi gembustsu – go to the source, observe first-hand the problems. Walk the gemba and speak to the users /operators to understand their issues. A good way to gather this information on the process is to complete a simple Value Stream Map (VSM).

2) Bring the operators to the analysis discussions. This is done for two reasons. A) They know what the problems are and probably have some good ideas for the solutions; and B) You will get better engagement from the team both throughout this process and in normal day to day activity. This approach will also give them their

opportunity to challenge the process and the solutions. It is important you give them the opportunity to challenge and listen to their concerns; do not ignore their concerns, you never know, you may uncover some real talent. I believe the best ideas come from the operators themselves; sometimes the ideas may need to be expanded or combined however the operators generally know the solutions.

3) Also bring other parts of the business to the analysis discussions. Fresh eyes often come up with fresh ideas and they are not working from the habits that can be seen in every part of every business. Select the teams for the discussions carefully, you want to have a good cross section of people that will all bring something to the discussion and be mindful of the quieter or less confident participants; they may require some prompting to get their ideas, however that extra work is often very much worth the effort.

4) Follow the Plan, Do, Check, Act (PDCA) cycle when implementing the process changes. Remember, the outcomes from the analysis should eliminate the risk so there will be some changes to the way the operators work. Provide instructions, training and be patient. Check regularly and methodically to ensure the results are as expected and that it hasn't added waste or OHS risks.

Bring the team back together as often as possible during the early period of the implementation to discuss the changes and get subjective feedback to support the objective data. This is an important step as the people involved in the process play a big part in the success or failure of the process and organisation. Having positive objective data to show the process is successful is all very good and vital to capture but it's also critical for the sustainability of the change to measure or promote the softer benefits such as reduced frustration, improved staff engagement etc.

5) Recognition of the team is the final step (before starting over with the next opportunity). I'm not a fan of rewarding what should be normal activity, however recognition is a valuable tool that when applied effectively can further improve the engagement of the team involved and the broader business.

Let's now take a look at some pokayoke success stories. I have modified the following case studies so as to remove any link to the business or individuals, however all of these stories have been collected first hand from either my involvement or from interviewing those involved first hand.

Case 1.

Problem:

The incorrect component was being welded onto the assembly consistently with the resulting finished part being unsuitable for use.

Outcome:

Scrap material

Solution:

Pokayoke design to eliminate the risk of incorrect parts being assembled. By design, the part will not fit through the use of notching and tabs.

Case 2.

Problem:

Parts consistently missing from packaged components and accessories. These were small parts and fasteners.

Outcome:

Customer dissatisfaction due to inconvenience of not being able to complete installation. Risk of business losing customers.

Solution:

This solution came from an operator facing the problem and frustration every day. A jig was designed to hold the parts prior to packaging. The parts then fell through the jig into the bag; only when all parts were in place was the operator able to release the parts to the chute.

Case 3.

Problem:

Inconsistent coverage of coconut on a conveyor due to the distribution of coconut on the spreader being thin towards the outer edges. When adjusted perfectly the spreader would function well, however the adjustments were very fine and difficult to perfect.

Outcome:

Scrap product from the outer edges.

Solution:

The solution was to narrow the conveyor slightly on both outer edges to ensure the usable area received consistent coverage. This did result in reduced throughput, however did considerably reduce the wastage and labour utilized for sorting.

Some simple solutions that can be seen in every household include:

- Electrical plugs. Countries or regions using different voltage or amperage have different shaped plugs that cannot be inserted into the wrong voltage sockets.
- Pepper shakers have less holes than salt shakers to reduce risk of over seasoning.
- Most motorcycles will not allow a gear to be engaged when the side stand is down to eliminate the risk of accident caused by riding with the stand down.
- An SD card cannot be inserted the incorrect way due to the design of the card and corresponding slot.

There are many, many more that could possibly fill a book by itself but I think the above examples provide sufficient evidence that pokayoke is everywhere and isn't restricted to manufacturing. It can be more challenging to implement pokayoke in the office or service environment, however with the right approach, people and attitude it can be achieved successfully. Using different sized paper for important forms and receptacles of the same size is one method that can be used in the office. Another is the use of electronic eyes or scanners for important documents to be recorded into the IT system. This can eliminate the risk of keying errors and greatly reduce the frequency of data errors (the scanners are improving but are still not perfect).

3. Statistical Analysis

Statistical analysis plays an important role in the application of quality in ensuring those issues that are of most importance are the issues that are prioritized. In many organisations (probably most) the loudest issue; that is the issue creating the most noise in the business is the issue prioritized highest. Data often shows these issues are not always the most critical and therefore should not be prioritized as high.

This is the reason an effective system relies on data collection and analysis. There are many books and websites on this subject and the purpose of this chapter is not to provide an in-depth detailed guide but to provide an overview of the statistical measurements that can assist in the implementation of a lean business system. This chapter also isn't about Six Sigma. Six Sigma has its place and can be a valuable method, however I prefer to use the method and philosophy of lean with a mix of statistical analysis when and where necessary.

Although not precisely statistical analysis, the basic tools of quality below support and further enable statistical process control. With the use of these tools you can develop an effective quality measurement and analysis system and culture. The quality system and certification is discussed in more detail in a later chapter.

The Nine Basic Tools of Quality

The nine basic tools of quality provide a simple set of tools that when used effectively can enable an organisation to monitor its performance and conduct root cause analysis to improve its processes. The origin of the tools is diverse, however many of the principles have been derived from the work of W. Edwards Deming.

Cause and Effect Diagram

The cause and effect diagram is also known as a Fishbone or Ishikawa Diagram. Fishbone after the shape of the object and Ishikawa after Kaoru Ishikawa who developed the tool.

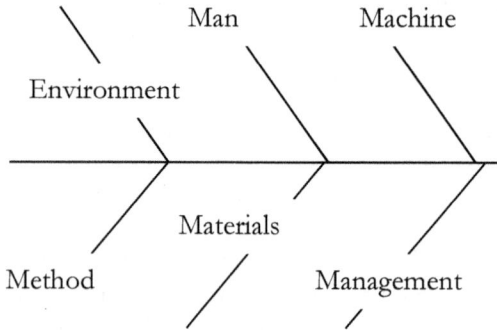

The causes are usually grouped into:

- Man
- Method
- Machine
- Materials
- Management
- Environment (Mother nature)

This gives us the 6 M's used in manufacturing. Marketing use a similar process named the 7 P's:

- Product / Service
- Price

- Place
- Promotion
- People
- Positioning
- Packaging

It is essential that the group completing the exercise have a good working understanding of the process being analysed. It can also be beneficial to include a cross functional team to gain from different experiences and objectives. The diagram is used to identify all of the potential causes for a result (usually a non-conformance, however can be used to replicate a good result) and is quite easy to complete by branching off from the main branches as you add more causes against each heading. You may not always identify causes for every heading or you may have quite a number for each.

I use the Ishikawa in conjunction with the next tool, 5 Why's as I find the Ishikawa helps identify the possible causes to be further analysed with the next tool.

5 Why's

The 5Why's is simply asking the question "Why" enough times to identify the root cause of the problem. The root cause is the underlying cause that when fixed will result in the elimination of the problem with no reoccurrence.

When the root cause is not fixed you are simply reacting to symptoms and will see the problem repeated. This will likely lead to increased costs and increased unplanned downtime due to the higher frequency of occurrence. The 5 Why's can be used to analyse any problem whether it is quality, efficiency, safety, breakdown etc.

The first step of conducting 5 Why analysis is to clearly define the problem; this is where I find the Ishikawa helpful as it can narrow down the starting point. The Ishikawa can also give you a couple of places to start and I often use the 5 Why's on each.

Example:

Problem: Fuse blown on wet saw.

Why? Pump overloaded.

Why? Lack of lubrication

Why? Pump pressure too low.

Why? Pump shaft is worn.

Why? Metal shavings are sucked up into pump.

Why? No filter on pump.

Without applying the 5 Why's the fuse would have been replaced over and over before it was realized that the lubrication was poor. This may have led to overfilling the lubrication reservoir or replacing the pump. When in fact the root cause was a lack of filter on the pump intake which could be a design defect, failure or maintenance issue.

Check Sheet

The simple checksheet if often overlooked and seen as "old fashioned". I would disagree and believe the checksheet still has an important role to play in business. The format may change and the technology is shifting toward electronic forms and applications however the purpose remains unchanged. That purpose is to provide a simple method of monitoring the inputs, activity and outputs of any business process.

I am still using checksheets today, although I use a tablet computer and a template in place of paper and pen As I write this chapter I am also preparing a presentation on Quality Management to a group of 120; earlier today I drafted the presentation and I am using 3 different checksheets to show the audience how an effective quality system looks; checksheets provide the evidence.

Control Charts

A control chart is used to monitor the performance over time. In the field of quality statistical process control (SPC) it monitors the parts within specification tolerances and the variation of production outputs. It is necessary to know the upper and lower design limits; this gives you the overall tolerance of the design.

In the above example the UCL signifies the Upper Control Limit and the LCL signifies the Lower Control Limit. The X line shows the process output over the sample; in this example the sample size is ten. The example shows a process lacking control. This is evidenced by samples four and six being above the UCL. Through further analysis, you can see that after three samples above or at the UCL (samples 4, 5 & 6) the following sample is found to be at the LCL before finishing at the mid point. This indicates the operator was not certain how to bring the process back in control so made an over-correction at sample 7. If the process was better controlled, when sample 4 was found to be above the UCL the operator would have had a clear method of correction. A larger sample size and higher frequency of sampling will provide better data for analysis.

Histogram

A histogram is another chart used to display the distribution of data; it is sometimes called a distribution chart. Unlike the control chart, a histogram uses a column chart rather than line. In a mathematical sense, a histogram can be quite complex however when used in SPC it is often made quite simple to show a single trend. When developing a histogram it is necessary to have quite a large sample size. This is due to each column indicating the frequency of that outcome occurring. When a small sample size is used the chart will appear quite flat or narrow peaks.

In the above example the spread is as you would expect from a reasonably controlled process. You generally do not include the LCL and UCL in a histogram as you are interested in the distribution. If you find the distribution forms a nice bell curve but is achieving out of spec parts you can adjust the mid-point settings of the machinery to move the entire curve without causing the process to go out of control.

Pareto Chart

The pareto chart was developed by Vilfredo Pareto and shows the values in descending order from the left vertical axis by columns. It is often referred to when discussing the 80/20 rule; this is not the purpose of the chart but is an often seen result that 80% of the total is derived from 20% of the values. For this reason, a second vertical axis is often used to indicate the running percentage via a line chart.

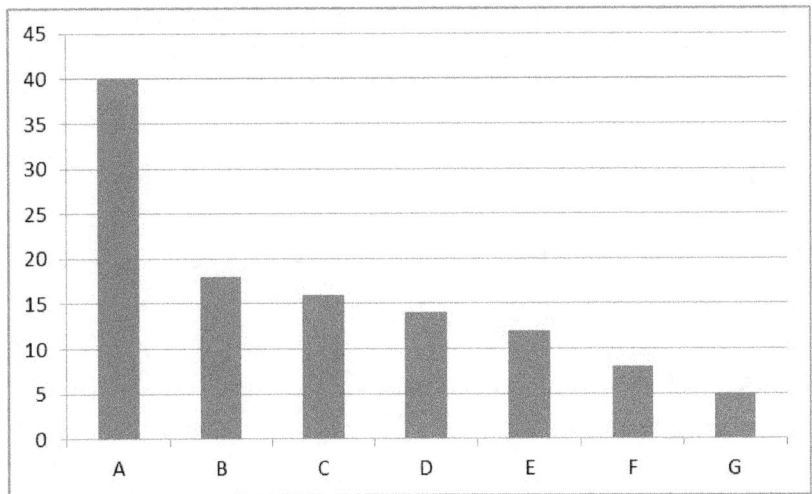

The above example is a basic pareto chart without a secondary vertical axis. I usually don't use the secondary vertical axis as for the purpose I use the pareto for it isn't necessary. I use the pareto to simply indicate the frequency of issues to then focus efforts on the issue with the higher frequency rather than focus on the 'loudest problem".

Scatter Diagram

The scatter chart is another chart used in the analysis of data. It can be used to analyse a number of variables and is always used to plot two variables (X and Y). I have used the scatter diagram to analyse the cut pattern of a pack saw to determine the optimum setting to achieve the greatest number of parts within spec. A pack saw is an automatic band saw that cuts an entire (or part thereof) pack of steel or timber. In the example I used the scatter chart the saw was cutting packs of steel containing 24 lengths of SHS.

We had issues where the number of non-conforming parts produced was far too high. The issue was compounded as we identified part both above and below the control limits. The upper limit being 1149.50mm and the lower limit 1148.5mm; an overall tolerance of 1.0mm. The saw design accuracy was a cut within 0.5mm.

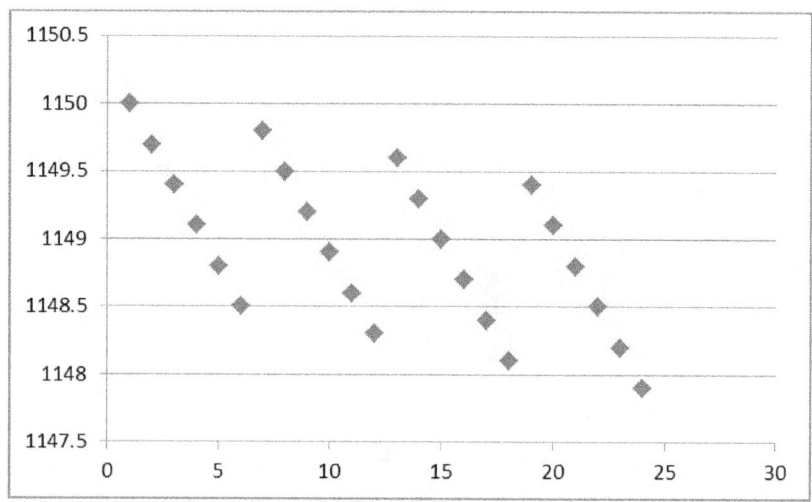

When we plotted the results in the scatter diagram we were presented with an obvious trend. The saw was cutting at and angle from left to right and a further angle from top to bottom. Through further investigation we identified an incorrect alignment to be the cause of the left to right angle cut and an inferior blade selection for the material being cut to be the cause of the angle cut from top to bottom. After the modifications were completed the below chart resulted.

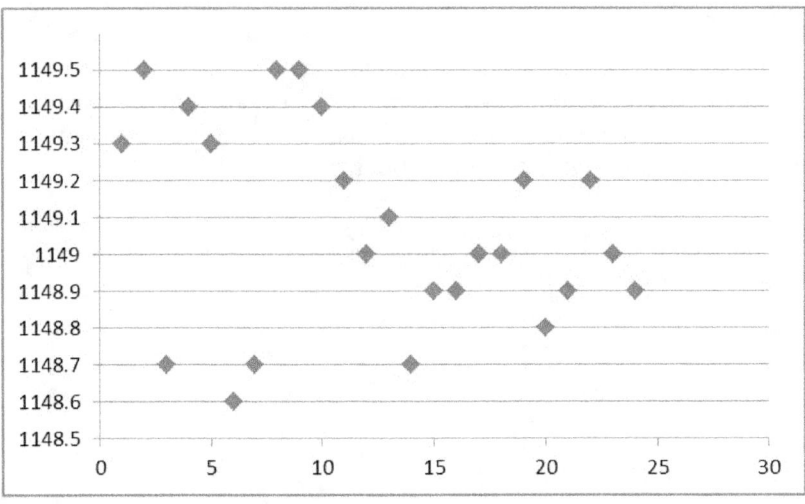

The above chart represents a random distibution of an in control process. This example shows the outcome after adjustments were made to the pack saw.

Flow Chart

Most people have seen or developed a flow chart these days and they really are a simple tool that can be very effective in communicating a process. In fact, the more simple the better really. The most effective way to develop your flow charts is to keep it as simple as possible. A flow chart needs to be easily read and understood if it is to be used as a training and auditing tool. There are two main types of flow charts:

1) Basic flow chart

These are a single column or row and contain the entire process flow within one frame.

2) Deployment flow chart

These are also called swim lanes as the process is divided into lanes of responsibility.

There is no right or wrong way. I prefer deployment flow charts for any process involving more than a single department or area of responsibility. I may use a basic flow chart when the responsibility is handed over cleanly and does not rebound.

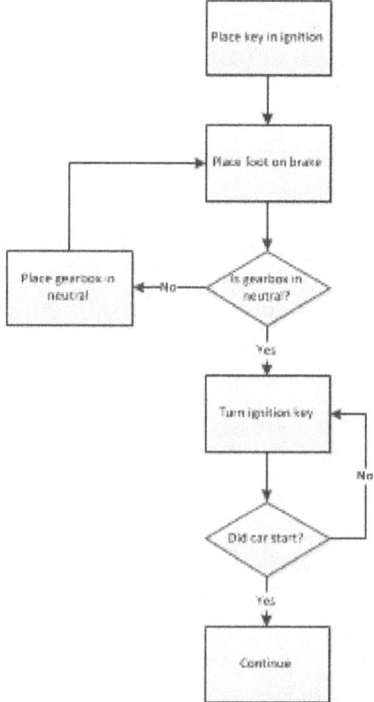

The above basic flowchart shows the process of starting a regular car engine. The process steps are indicated by rectangles and any questions within the process are indicated by diamonds with loops where necessary. The basic flow chart is a good choice for such simple processes however can become messy and difficult to follow when the process becomes more complex. This is where a deployment flow chart becomes necessary.

Run Chart

A run chart is similar to a control chart in that the sample results are plotted on a line chart. However whereas a control chart plots this data against the upper and lower control limits, a run chart only plots the results and a trending line.

The run chart is more suitable for larger run samples over a longer time period to determine the capability of a process over this timeframe.

CPK

Cpk is one of a number of formulae of process capability index and is used to estimate what a process is likely to produce. Cpk considers that the mean result may not be within the control limits. The Cp formula does not and considers only that the results are distributed evenly between the control limits.

I use the Cpk value for most of the work I do, however you can use whichever best suits your purposes. SPC can work on high or low volume operations, however a failure in a lower volume operation will have a greater impact on the results than a larger volume sample size.

If you are interested in further information, formulae and instructions on SPC I would recommend a more detailed text type publication as the topic is quite detailed and outside of the scope of this book.

4. PPAP

WHAT IS PPAP?

PPAP is an acronym for Production Part Approval Process and is a process used largely in the Automotive Industry to control the approval of new suppliers and new designs prior to entering full production status. This reduces the potential for design and/or systemic manufacturing issues to be identified during normal production and greatly reduces the potential for recalls. Although PPAP was developed for and is mostly used in automotive it can be used in any business and is effective for manufacturing and service with some modification to the process.

PPAP is the approval submission of the Advanced Product Quality Planning (APQP). The forms and documents are published by the Automotive Industry Action Group (AIAG).

APQP FORMS

The PPAP consists of the following APQP forms and documents. As the forms are the copyright property of AIAG we will not be providing examples, however will discuss the purpose and scope of the documents. Not all of the below forms are required for a PPAP submission and not all will benefit every situation. An agreed submission for each situation is the best way to approach an internal PPAP. If the document isn't going to add value then why waste time completing; be cautious though, don't confuse waste with "too difficult". Look at the consequences of not doing the work, if they are significant then the work should probably be done.

Below is a list of common APQP documents in a PPAP submission:

DFMEA and associated checklists

Design matrix

Tool checklist

Quality checklist

Floor layout checklist

Characteristic matrix

Flowcharts and checklist

PFMEA and checklist

Control Plan and checklist

Inspection test reports

As you can see, it is quite a comprehensive list of documents. Now we will spend a little time going through each one and discuss its use and benefits.

DFMEA and associated checklists

Design Failure Mode Effect Analysis is used early in the design phase to identify potential failures in the product design. It is a critical step or gate in the design process and should include cross functional analysis of past designs and proposed designs. The DFMEA is similar to a risk assessment in that it looks at the risk, likelihood and severity. The score is called an RPN; the lower the score the greater the probability of success of the design.

Design matrix

The design matrix is used prior to the DFMEA and is used as an input document. The design matrix is simply a list of known potential causes of failures; these causes are then given a ranking of 0-3 based on appearance, performance, process ability and environmental failure modes. This information then provides input to the DFMEA for failure modes.

Some may think this is a double up of review, however when done correctly does not add too much time if any as the next step of the process is made easier and faster with this information.

Tool checklist

The tool checklist is used to provide a level of confidence that the design team have determined, designed and developed all of the specific tooling requirements to enable the consistent manufacture of the new design prior to implementation. The checklist can often include sign-off for the testing and SPC audit of the equipment.

Some of the important aspects of a tool checklist are:

- Quick die change
- Pokayoke
- Repeatability control
- Volume independent

Quality checklist

This is a checklist for the entire process and is used as part of the pre PPAP submission check to ensure all required documents and aspects have been completed / submitted. This checklist includes checks on design, assessment, layout, training, documentation for production, gauging, inwards goods and more. It is a very comprehensive one page checklist for the business.

Floor layout checklist

Used in conjunction with the tool checklist, the floor layout checklist provides a pre-implementation analysis of the best floor layout to support the effective manufacture of the design. The floor layout checklist includes analysis of the best material flow and optimum resourcing of the production facility to achieve the required processing parameters.

Characteristic matrix

This is a very simple matrix designed to assist with the inspection of critical characteristics of the product both for pre-production and production runs. The critical aspects (usually dimensions) are listed and numbered with description, tolerances and recording section to record actual results measured.

Flowcharts and checklist

Every new product requires revised flowcharts for the internal processing, cross functional interactions and external support. A systems view is a valuable tool to identify the high level interactions and provide an understanding of the flowchart requirements. A flowchart should be developed for all interactions required for the product realization.

PFMEA and checklist

Process Failure Mode Effect Analysis (PFMEA) is similar to the DFMEA and is used to preview and analyse the process rather than the design. It looks at the process in detail (step by step) and rates the steps and alternatives of the processing to provide a level of confidence to the implementation team.

Control Plan and checklist

The Control Plan (also called Production Control Plan or PCP) is developed for every product being manufactured. It is not designed to be a work instruction however, it does show the critical steps of the process. The PCP provides key characteristics of the product at each process step and normally requires sign-off at each step and often doubles as a recording sheet for the key characteristic results.

Inspection test reports

Inspection test reports are used throughout the design and development process to capture key information of product conformance. An ITR will usually be submitted after the initial prototype, the pre-production, and the first-off production stages. These are submitted as part of the PPAP documentation.

Other documents such as Gage R&R, Finish / Appearance Inspection, Material Inspection are used where required to provide the customer with confidence of the process reliability.

5. Standards

Of the standards applied to quality systems and their implementation, the most widely used is ISO 9001. I won't be going into the history of this standard in this book however will be discussing the benefits and otherwise of the use of this standard in your business.

ISO 9001 is the international standard for Quality Management Systems (QMS); there are corresponding guidelines and implementation manuals published and distributed by your local standards body. ISO 9001 is a set of guidelines developed to assist businesses in the development of their own set of policies, procedures and supporting documentation and systems to effectively operate to best practice. The term "best practice" is often thrown around in the world of business; but what does it really mean? To me, it means that a business can operate at its optimum efficiency, effectiveness and is a leader in its field of endeavour or expertise.

While the use of benchmarking can be of some benefit, it is my belief that too much emphasis is put on this activity; rather than benchmarking regularly a business should benchmark at startup or early in its life as a gap analysis tool to assist the development of its systems. From that point they can choose to adopt the guidelines of ISO 9001 to provide a robust and documented business operating system.

There are two points in the above paragraph that need to be further expanded upon.

1) It isn't absolutely necessary to achieve certification to have an effective QMS

2) A QMS can be and should be more than just a QMS; for a QMS to be most effective it must be fully integrated into the organisation. It must be more than just a QMS.

Certification

There is no doubt about the benefits of achieving certification to a standard. These include:

- An external audit and inspection of your systems to ensure not only compliance but also to provide valuable feedback.

- A competitive advantage over uncertified competitors. This is very market driven.

- Internally, certification can have the effect of increasing buy-in across the organisation as some employees see the system as compliant and therefore "better".

Certification is not the right direction for every business though. In some instances developing a compliant system without undergoing certification is the right approach. This can be due to a number of reasons, including:

- Lack of market requirement. This can be countered by a business having the desire to be a groundbreaker in their market. Once this occurs they may enjoy a strong advantage while the competition plays catch up. It must be said however that some markets just have no demand for certification.

- Limited resources to manage a certified system. Certification will add cost to a business; it is my belief though that an effective system will more than cover this cost through increased efficiencies and reduced waste.

- Lack of available funds to undertake the certification audits. This should be seen as a temporary situation and is a common approach in smaller businesses. Develop the systems at stage 1, prove the systems over a period of time and continue to achieve certification at stage 2.

There is no single right way to achieve certification. The following approach is one I have used on a number of occasions for the effective design and implementation of a certified Quality Management System.

Step 1) A knowledgeable operator conducts an initial audit of the current systems and processes against the standard. This audit is performed on the "raw" systems to understand exactly where the business is in its journey toward certification.

Step 2) Analyse the audit results and perform a gap analysis. This is done by comparing the audit results against the standard requirements. This process needs to be very rigorous to provide the business with the best chance of achieving certification at its first attempt and thereby reduce the costs associated with external audits.

Step 3) Go about developing the systems, processes and documentation to close off every gap identified in the initial audit. This is the longest stage of the process and really cannot be rushed. For the system to be effective, it must be tailored to the organisation. It isn't a one size fits all but must be relevant to and specific to each organisation.

Step 4) Implement and train the system across the organisation. You cannot pass certification if the processes are on paper and not trained or in use across the business. The processes must be embedded and effectively trained.

Step 5) Conduct a second internal audit by the same operator as the initial audit or a similarly trained and experienced operator. It is unlikely this audit will achieve a perfect result; this is the point of a second internal audit. You will have to go back to the systems, processes and documentation again to close out any final gaps.

Step 6) Finally, when you are confident of your chances of success you should organise an external audit.

The internal audits can be conducted by your certification partner if you choose and for the inexperienced operator this is probably a good idea. It will add significantly to the expense though. The costs of certification can be quite high so it is recommended to obtain quotes prior to taking too big a step.

QMS

The documentation required for a QMS will be discussed in the next chapter, however it is important to expand on point 2 from this chapter.

A business can become certified to ISO 9001 by implementing a stand-alone QMS, but to get the most out of the system and the investment, a QMS should be fully integrated into and across the organisation. This is an area I am quite passionate about and have in the past turned down work based on the organisations lack of integration.

I have experienced, and I'm sure many of the readers have also, organisations that are certified to ISO 9001 or any other standard yet when dealing with them in any capacity you are left questioning how they could have achieved certification. There are a number of reasons how this situation could occur, not least that their certification organisation has pretty low standards.

My point here is that certification itself does not ensure your business will operate at a high level. It takes integration into the business and a commitment to compliance internally, without relying on external auditing to maintain compliance, for the system to be effective and achieve its intent. For this reason, more important than being certified is to develop a system with checks, robust auditing and timely management reviews built in; these are all requirements of certification however are easily bluffed unfortunately. Only when the organisation shows this level of commitment will their system add value rather than cost other than marketing value.

My recommendation to business owners and boards to ensure their system is as effective as possible is to request different auditors from their external audit provider each audit. This way the auditors do not become complacent or used to the organisation and its system and will therefore be more robust.

The golden rule is simple: certification is not just a marketing tool, but is a process to ensure your organisation's systems and processes are compliant and robust to provide an effective management system which results in a sustainable business model.

6. Documentation

ISO 9001 does not contain an absolute list of required documents, it does however provide the requirements that your documentation must respond to and manage. As the standard matures it is good to see the expectations for documentation are becoming leaner. The 2015 revision is looking like following this trend.

Even though the standard does not provide a list of documents, there are two absolute requirements and a number of documents that are regarded as the basic set.

Quality Policy

This is a requirement for ISO 9001 and every business should have a quality policy regardless of their certification intentions. The quality policy is a high level document providing interested parties an understanding of what the business does and how it intends to ensure quality outputs to meet the customer needs and expectations. In a hierarchy of documents, the quality policy sits beneath the company vision and missions statements.

The quality policy is often one of the only external documents (not forms) of the QMS and is usually displayed in the foyer or reception area to be available for interested parties and provides a marketing opportunity for potential clients and customers to see.

Quality Manual

Like the policy, the manual is a requirement in the current revision of ISO 9001. There is no definitive right or wrong manual; however below are some of the core features of a quality manual.

- The QMS scope, any exclusions and the design of the system.
- A diagrammatic view of the QMS and documentation.
- Business overview: a brief overview of what the business does, how it achieves its purpose and the long term strategy

of the business. I would include a diagrammatical view of the business in the way of a Systems View diagram of similar; a high level process map can also be an effective means of showing the interactions.

- Organisation structure: this can be complemented by organisation charts to show the different parts of the organisation and the management structure. This is also where you should show how the business supports its QMS from a human resource perspective.

Document Control

This should be the first procedure developed for your QMS as it will define how all other documents are written, named, controlled and stored.

Your document control procedure will include instructions on the naming convention used in your business. This convention needs to enable any user of the system to identify where in the business the document is in use. Control of documents is an important feature of any QMS and should clearly indicate the currency of all documents.

Management Review

This is another important document and is used to define how and when the organisation will review its QMS.

Resource Management

This includes human resources, infrastructure and the work environment. This document needs to define how the organisation determines the competencies and training requirement to ensure customer satisfaction.

Product Realization

These documents are used to define how the organisation will control the design, development and production of its product or service. This also includes the supply chain processes used to support the operations. Quite often a number of documents are used to cover this section of the standard.

Measurement, Analysis and Improvement

These documents detail how the organisation monitors customer satisfaction, internal auditing and general measurement of performance. This also includes how the organisation controls non-conforming product and continual improvement; including preventive and corrective actions.

In addition to the above, the QMS will include many other supporting documents such as; procedures, work instructions and forms used in the organisation to ensure compliance to internal and external requirements and customer satisfaction.

www.ingramcontent.com/pod-product-compliance
Lightning Source LLC
Chambersburg PA
CBHW051734170526
45167CB00002B/930